Ella and Ethan's Christmas List

Mary O'Keeffe

It was a few weeks before **Christmas**.

There was lots to do to get **ready**.

Mam had a big list of jobs.

Dad said that Mam was a bit like **Santa** with her list!

"Any more jobs for me to do?" he asked.

"Yes," said Mam. "I want you to get the **Christmas** tree down next."

Ella and I were busy.

I laid down my pen and pad.

I had to do up a list as well, but my list was for **Santa**!

"I do not want to wait for **Christmas**!" said Ella with a moan.

"Be good or you will get a bag of coal!" I said.

She just had to wait. So did I!

"Can I peep at your list, Ella?" I asked.

Ella had a doll that you can feed milk to, a soft cat with a long tail and a foam soap set on her list.

What do I pick? What do I ask for?

In the end, I put down a few bits and bobs.

It did not have loads on it, but it was my best **Christmas** list ever!

Dad got the **Christmas** tree box down.

The box was big.

It was hard to lift.

Dad gave a big yelp.
We had to go fast!
Oh no!
The box fell where I had laid my list!

"Are you all okay?" said Mam with a wail.

"I have a pain in my leg!" Dad wept.

He bent down to look at his heel.

"It will mend," he said.

Ella gave him a hug.

"My list for **Santa** is torn," I cried, "and my pen is bent. It will not work."

I can **post** my **Christmas** cards while we are there.

"We need to put a new job on my list," said Mam. "Let's go down to the **post office**, Evan. We can do a new list and then put yours and Ella's in the post box for **Santa**."

We got in the car and got on the road to the **post office**.

There were loads from the town there!

There were so many that Mam and I did not see where to go.

Then a man from the **post office** saw us.

"Do you need any help?" he asked.

"You are like **Santa's** little elf!" said Mam.

The man gave me a pen and a new pad.

I sat at the desk and did my **Christmas** list again.

Mam paid at the till and then we put the lists in the red post box for **Santa**.

"**Ready**? Let's go and see what Dad and Ella are up to now!" said Mam.

"How long before the post gets to **Santa**?" I asked.

"We will just have to wait and see!" said Mam with a wink.